Kindness

Journal

6 MINUTES A DAY
TO YOUR HAPPIEST YOU

The *Kindness* Journal

6 MINUTES A DAY
TO YOUR HAPPIEST YOU

CREATED BY

NATASHA SHARMA

Dedication

To my babies,
Jay and Dane.
May you grow to always be
kind, compassionate, and loving.

And to all those who
strive to be better and improve,
shake things up, and move.
You change the world.

My religion is very simple. My religion is kindness.

– Dalai Lama

10 Things You'll Love About *The Kindness Journal*

The Kindness Journal is the easiest and most powerful way to happiness.

It will genuinely improve your life in just minutes a day.

It's a Guided Journal for people who don't want to stare at an empty page and pour out their thoughts.

It looks simple, but each entry is carefully curated based on the science and wisdom of Positive Psychology for maximum impact.

The Kindness Journal focuses on your strengths, virtues, and behaviors that are proven to be effective in achieving growth and enrichment.

You'll feel a difference after a single day, let alone four months.

If you're old enough to read it and write down your answers, this journal is for you!

Being kind is not a cure-all. It won't get you into an Ivy League college, make you CEO of a fortune 500 company, or bring you fame.

But it will make you the best and happiest version of *you*.

And that makes everything else *infinitely* more possible.

Contents

The
Kindness
Journal

6 MINUTES A DAY
TO YOUR HAPPIEST YOU

Kindness and Happiness 101

Remember there's no such thing as a small act of kindness. Every act creates a ripple with no logical end. — **Scott Adams**

Chances are when you were growing up you heard a lot of advice coming from a lot of people. Repeatedly. Things like "Sit up straight", "Say please", "Say thank you", and my personal favorite, "Be good." When you think about it, nobody ever really teaches us or asks us to "Be kind."

When I became a mother a few years ago, a friend asked me what I would want most for my son to be. After thinking about it, I surprised myself with this reply: "I want him to be healthy, independent, and kind."

Let's face a few facts. It's the quest for happiness that is an important and natural goal for almost everyone, not kindness. And with good reason! Research has shown that the ability to be happy and content with life plays a central role in positive mental health. So it's pretty understandable why most of us are looking for ways to increase that feeling as much as possible.

How do we become happier?

And there it is, the million-dollar question. It is only recently that we have been asking it of ourselves, along with how we can become happier. Older approaches to mental wellness focused on identifying abnormal behavior and attempting to cure it. We've come a long way since then.

Positive psychology is the first approach to our well being that focuses on how we can flourish in our own skin. It emphasizes individual strengths and how we can feel more fulfilled, instead of on our weaknesses and shortfalls. It looks at the 'how' of happiness.

In a nutshell, a person's happiness is determined by three main things:

- A person's unique set point for happiness
- Circumstances that are related to happiness
- Activities that are related to happiness[1]

A set point refers to a genetic tendency toward a certain level of happiness that each of us is born with. You could call it our disposition or temperament. We can fluctuate around the baseline, but eventually we return to our natural set point. So are we all stuck on being 'set' in our ways? Or can we achieve and sustain a level of happiness that is higher than our set point? You bet we can! Read on.

Circumstances refer to things in our environment or lives that contribute to our level of happiness. These can include such things as where you live, your age, gender, social status and involvement, income level, and personal experiences. We can control and influence some of these things, but not all of them. In addition, they are only minor influencers when it comes to our happiness.

By far the easiest and most powerful way to influence our own individual well being is through intentional actions that we commit to practicing. In fact research has shown that this can determine our level of happiness by up to 40%![2]

What are intentional actions?

An intentional action is one that we do consciously and with purpose.

Everyday experiences have shown us that our emotions rule. They cause us to act in certain ways. In the field of cognitive-behavioral psychology, we have known for years that our cognitions (thoughts, beliefs, and attitudes) have the power to shape our emotions. As an example, if we believe we are a fundamentally likeable person we are likely to feel more positive emotions and act accordingly. Conversely if we believe we are generally unlikeable, we will probably experience more negative emotions - like sadness or anxiety - and our actions and behavior will reflect that feeling.

Here's the good news: We have the ability to act intentionally and control our beliefs, and therefore control our emotions. This involves becoming aware of what those beliefs are, then challenging them, and finally changing them if they are untrue.

Here's the even better news: This works in reverse as well with actions, and arguably even better. If we intentionally act in more positive ways, we are likely to feel more uplifted and fulfilled and carry a similar attitude toward the world. If we act in more negative ways, we have a better chance of feeling down, depressed, and see the world through a lackluster lens.

Why a kindness journal?

What exactly is kindness?

Kindness is the practice of being considerate, caring, affectionate and generous in spirit.

You can exercise kindness in two ways: Toward yourself, and toward others. Let's take a closer look.

Being kind to yourself can look like a lot of different things. Treating yourself to your favorite food or drink, watching your favorite movie again, hanging out with a great friend, or taking a much-needed break in the form of a vacation or a simple nap.

You can also express self-kindness by doing things like forgiving yourself for something you did in the past, setting healthy boundaries in relationships, or letting go of painful memories and experiences in your life.

When you are kind to yourself you're not just helping yourself to feel happy, you are helping others too. When you feel happy and well, you'll be better at everything to everyone around you: A better son, daughter, brother, sister, mother, father, student, employee, friend, girlfriend, boyfriend, wife, husband, and so on.

There are lots of simple acts of kindness that you can practice. Contrary to popular belief, they don't have to be random, anonymous, or big. In fact, they have the most effect when they are planned and very much on purpose. These can include things like helping a fellow classmate with their homework, carrying someone's grocery bags for them to their car, or writing someone a thank you note. People at the receiving end of kind acts feel more connected and are inspired to act with more kindness themselves.

In addition when you are kind to others, you're not just helping them you're helping yourself too. In a study conducted by Sonja Lyubomirsky at University of California Riverside, students were asked to perform five acts of kindness per week for a period of six weeks. At the end of the study, the students reported feeling nearly *42% happier* than before.[3]

Kindness to you is kindness to me; kindness to me is kindness to you.

- Rick Hanson

Benefits of practicing kindness.

- More positive state of being
- Stronger relationships and feeling more connected to others
- Higher self-esteem
- Higher compassion and empathy
- More confidence
- Increased sense of cooperation
- Higher sense of meaning and purpose in life
- Better social rewards
- Better awareness and appreciation of what you have
- Increased creativity
- Increased productivity
- More physical energy
- Better self-regulation and self-control
- Reduced feelings of depression, anxiety, and stress

Conclusion? **Being kind has a deeply positive effect on happiness.**

A quick note here about seeking happiness: Not all of life's moments can be happy ones, and this journal isn't about making you believe that you can feel positive and happy all of the time. Every emotion has its place and value in our lives. It's about balance.

We live in the fastest paced society in the history of the world. Unfortunately, our brain's ability to process the world has not increased in the same proportion. We all have happy moments in life, but too often they are easily forgotten in the busyness of our daily schedules. What if we could channel those positive feelings and make them last for weeks, months, or better yet, all of the time? If we could accomplish that it would lead us to feelings of contentment and peace of mind. And that can last a lifetime, no matter what is happening around you.

The Building Blocks of Change

You will never change your life until you change something you do daily.
– John C. Maxwell

Quite often, it is the smallest things we do in a day that add up to have the most stunning impact to our overall lives. I've already mentioned that intentional actions have the ability to greatly influence our happiness. Research on the habits of some of the most successful entrepreneurs and accomplished athletes clearly supports the value of positive actions and rituals, consistently implemented amidst the chaos of our modern lives. The benefits of doing so include improved focus and attention, as well as greater confidence and emotional stability. We have many routine aspects to our days, from brushing our teeth to eating meals. However not many of us have deliberately established daily positive practices that have the power to enrich our lives.

We first make our habits, and then our habits make us.
– John Dryden

If you've read this far, you are probably seriously motivated to change your life. You're ready to start choosing new behaviors to make it the best one that it can possibly be. Kudos to you! Pressing on...

Writing a journal every day has been proven to be one of the most effective and beneficial things you can add to your daily routine. And you don't need to make a huge time commitment to reap maximum rewards from it. In mere minutes a day not only will you create a happier sense of being, you will also have assembled a log of life's memorable moments that might otherwise have been forgotten forever.

The best time to write this journal is shortly before going to sleep, so you can reflect on your entire day. Keep it on your nightstand or somewhere else that's close at hand. No matter how your day went, writing this journal *every night* will help you to focus on your strengths, savor what went well in your day, and plan for how to make your world better tomorrow. It allows you to end each day with practicing kindness to yourself as well as others, easily and effectively. Talk about resting easy.

Another quick note here, this time about kindness: Being kind isn't about accepting everything that happens around you to try and be agreeable. It isn't about liking everyone you meet in life (you won't). It isn't about participating in detrimental or dead-end relationships for the sake of being nice. And it isn't about saying 'yes' to everyone. Being kind is about holding yourself, your choices, and your actions to a set of standards that allow you to move through life with class, grace, and peace of mind.

To create change, we need three things: Insight, Motivation, and Action.

The Magic Formula

Affirmative Action

Act like you expect to get into the end zone.
— Christopher Morley

What do Robert De Niro, Anne Hathaway, and Kate Winslet all have in common? Well the obvious answer is that they are all famous actors who have been recognized across the planet for their outstanding abilities in the field of acting. But they have something else in common. They are practitioners of a technique called Method Acting, an approach to acting where the actor tries to somehow actually live their character in life. It is arguably the secret that is behind some of the most powerful and moving performances on film.

In the 19th century, William James of Harvard University first discovered that our actions can cause our emotions. Smiling can make you feel happy, while frowning can make you feel sad. In psychology we call this principle "Acting As If." By acting as if you are a certain type of person, you become that person. In everyday speak you might have heard this as "fake it 'till you make it." But there's actual science behind it!

Let's look at a study led by Dana Carney of Columbia Business School where she split the participants into two groups. The people in the first group were placed into power poses. Some were seated at desks, with their feet up on the table, and asked to look upward and interlock their hands behind the back of their heads. The people in the second group were placed in poses that were associated with weakness. Some were asked to place their feet on the floor, hands in their laps, looking at the ground.

Just a single minute of power posing in the first group of people showed a tremendous boost in their confidence, as well as changes to the chemical make-up of their brains and bodies.[4]

Conclusion? **Focus on positive action, not just positive thinking.**

The Affirmative Action is a statement in the journal about how you want to be as if you were already that right now. Each time you write the affirmation, you groom yourself to start acting more like that in the present. Let's look at an example. Suppose you would like to be more outgoing with others, and feel less shy. You might write the following in this section of your journal:

I am friendly, confident, and enjoy chatting with others.

When done consistently, you will in fact start to act as if you are a friendly, outgoing person who isn't shy. In time you'll start to notice a change in how you feel and subsequently, how you think and who you become. There's really no big secret. If it worked for Robert De Niro, Anne Hathaway, and Kate Winslet, it will work for you too.

Here are some more examples of how this could look in your journal:

Samples:

I am warm and loving with my friends and family.

I am a hardworking student/team member.

When we act different, we can become different.

Things You Love About You

I didn't lose the gold. I won the silver.
— Michelle Kwan

Have you ever done really well on an exam, say scoring in the 90% range, but all you can focus on is the 10% you didn't get? How about delivering a spectacular presentation, but find yourself ruminating for hours or even days after over the one slide you screwed up on? You're in good company.

As humans, we are naturally biased to look for and fixate on the negatives or gaps in our lives. This had real value hundreds of years ago when just surviving in the outdoors was a bit more challenging. But in today's modern times, it's mostly outdated. Yet many of us continue to focus on the negative – even in relation to things we are good at! We need to be kinder to ourselves.

When you write down the things you are proud of in this part of the journal, you are noticing and keeping a record of your accomplishments. Listing accomplishments that you feel proud of builds confidence and self-esteem.

Here are some examples of how this could look in your journal:

Looking back on today, things I am proud of are…

Waking up before 8 am this morning.

Got the job I applied for 3 weeks ago.

Booked the photography class I have always wanted to take.

Getting accepted to the college I want to go to.

<u>*Completed one full month of this journal.*</u>

Notice how some of these accomplishments are bigger and some are smaller. List all of them, because all of them are what make you great.

Reliving Your Favorite Moment: The Mental Photograph

Every day may not be good, but there's something good in every day.
– Alice Morse Earle

How many times have you heard yourself or someone else say "Stop and smell the roses?" We hear it all the time, and most of us get the gist of what it means. But how many of us know why this saying started or what's actually behind it?

Turns out it's not just a cliché.

Traditional psychology focuses on how to cope with the negative aspects of life and how to make up for our weaknesses. This has some value to it but it usually means we are finding ways to just get by and survive, instead of really *thrive*. Positive psychology takes a different approach. It encourages us to recognize that there are both positive and negative aspects to life, but to consciously shift our focus and attention to the more positive ones.

Fred Bryant, a social psychologist at Loyola University in Chicago, first introduced the idea of 'Savoring.' The goal of savoring is to harness and extend the force of our positive emotions and experiences. By doing this, we can make them last longer and truly maximize the benefits that a pleasant experience in our life has on us. Here's how it works:

Let's say in the middle of a busy day, you manage to get out for lunch with a friend for an hour. You eat at a restaurant where the food is great, and have a lively and fulfilling conversation filled with lots of jokes and laughs. At the end of it you both hustle back to your desks, ready to get down to work. And the pleasure of the experience is forgotten in the hustle and bustle of your day.

When you write your favorite moment of the day in the journal, you allow the memory of it to come back. You sit back, close your eyes, and for one minute relive the experience in your mind all over again, like a movie. Except this time you're fully present in the moment, paying special attention to all the details. These could include how the food smelled, remembering how it tasted, what music was playing in the background, a particular joke your friend told, how nice the décor in the restaurant was, etc. In essence you're taking a mental photograph of the moment, increasing the chance you'll store the experience and the emotion into your long-term memory.

Here are some examples of how this could look in your journal:

My favorite moment of today was...

Lunch at Spice Route with Michelle.

Seeing a rainbow across the city skyline.

Reading together with my 3-year old son before his bedtime.

When my boss/teacher told me I did a great job.

Notice how simple the examples are. It's easier for us to remember and savor the 'spectacular' moments in life, like winning a big competition, graduating from university, or getting married. You can put those in too when they happen. But the main idea is to notice and savor the little things within the every day. With practice, you'll begin to see how effortless your ability to do this will become and the amazing effect it will have on how you feel.

Fine Tuning Your Antennae

How beautiful a day can be when kindness touches it.   **– George Elliston**

They may be harder to spot on some days than others, but most days contain at least one nice thing that someone else did for you - whether it was random, planned, intentional or unintentional. And no, not because they were paid to be nice to you! How often do we acknowledge or even notice these things, especially when they aren't so obvious?

As I mentioned earlier, people at the receiving end of kind acts feel more connected to others, build better relationships, and are inspired to act with more kindness themselves. They also feel thankful in the act of recognizing them. The feeling of thankfulness is pleasing and therefore a reward for the effort of noticing nice things around us. When our brain feels pleasure or 'rewarded' for something, it releases more of the neurotransmitter called Dopamine into our systems. And that increases the probability of doing the thing we felt rewarded for again. And again.

This entry of the journal focuses on raising your ability to take note of the kindness in others. Once again, they don't have to be big or blow your mind. They simply need to have made you feel good, or your day better or easier. Here are a few examples:

Someone who showed me kindness today was...

The stranger who smiled at me on the subway.

The guy who gave me the dollar I was short on at the checkout.

The woman who gave up her seat on the bus for my toddler and I.

The kid who held the door open for me.

In a world where watching the news can feel like watching a horror movie that never ends, and people are invariably rude and inconsiderate at times, it's important to remember that for the most part the world is actually a warm and nice place to be.

Making Tomorrow Better

How wonderful it is that nobody need wait a single moment before starting to improve the world.
— Anne Frank

We are now at the part of The Kindness Journal where you plan for the intentional act of kindness you will perform the following day. I've already mentioned the massive benefits that have been measured in study participants who consistently completed kind acts each day. The trick is how to make sure we do it.

In the late 1990's, two very famous psychologists named Philip Zimbardo and John Boyd studied the various "time zones" people live in: Past, present, and future. They found that those who regularly incorporate some focus on what lies ahead tend to shape their lives in the best ways possible.

When you write the entry for "How will I make tomorrow better?" each night, you're not only identifying with your 'future self,' you're committing to being your best and finding ways to look forward to the next day. Have you ever had a vacation planned and realized half the fun is the boost to your mood in the days leading up to it? This is the same idea, except you can have that tingly feeling of anticipation every day.

The first four entries of the journal are about expressing kindness toward yourself. "How will I make tomorrow better" is about expressing kindness toward others. Here are some examples:

How will I make tomorrow better?

Leave a thank you note on my coworker's desk.

Bring my friend/partner/mom/dad a coffee or tea in the morning.

Give a stranger or someone I know a compliment.

Keep your kind acts fresh and new. Studies have shown that kind acts that vary widely and frequently increase the overall impact to happiness. And wherever possible, make sure these acts aren't anonymous so that you can experience the person's reaction on the other side of them (usually warmth, pleasure, and gratitude).

When we're in a good place, performing kind acts every day will put a skip into our step. In our darker moments, performing them is healing and sometimes more restorative than any therapy or medication we may try.

Weekly Dares

Challenges are what make life interesting.
Overcoming them is what makes life
meaningful.   **– Joshua J. Marine**

Want to know the secret to feeling young at heart
forever? It's through constantly challenging ourselves in
small or big ways. The positive benefits from just facing
them are countless, whether we overcome them or not.
When we try new things, and even dare to do things that
seem a bit uncomfortable, we stay engaged with the
world around us. We can also find out just what we are
capable of, often to our own surprise and delight.

We all benefit from taking thoughtful risks in life. In
addition to maximizing our performance, creativity, and
innovation, challenging ourselves is where most of our
personal growth comes from.

Each week as part of the journal, you will come across
a page with a small but meaningful 'dare' for you to
complete that week. Think of them as little trials. Go for it,
and get out of your comfort zone! But most importantly,
have fun with it.

Sticking To It

So we already know now how the brain rewires itself in response to its perception of receiving a reward for something. It increases the desire and probability that we'll complete the rewarded action again.

This journal contains four months worth of entries. Ideally you will want to write this journal every single day in order to achieve maximum benefits. But we've all been in that spot before: The one where we pick up a new activity with zest and excitement…only to abandon it shortly afterward.

That won't be you! The best way to positively reinforce a behavior is to reward it frequently and consistently. And you're going to come up with the incentives for yourself. Here's an example of how it could look:

On completing the first week of this journal,
I will reward myself with…

A trip to the movies.

On completing the first month of this journal,
I will reward myself with…

Lunch or dinner at my favorite restaurant.

On completing the fourth month of this journal,
I will reward myself with…

A nice relaxing massage or a mini getaway.

Now it's your turn. In the lines following, fill in the specific things you will reward yourself with at each milestone:

On completing the first week of this journal,
I will reward myself with…

On completing the first month of this journal,
I will reward myself with…

On completing the fourth month of this journal,
I will reward myself with…

It's time for you to take the reins into your hands and start The Kindness Journal, the most important and effective step you can take to increase your personal happiness and well being. You have all the tools for success. You're ready.

My Journal

DATE _____ / _____ / 20 _____

The only impossible journey is the one you never begin.
- ANTHONY ROBBINS

I am...

I am friendly, confident, and enjoy chatting with others.

I am warm and loving with my friends and family.

I am a hardworking student/team member who puts forth my best.

Looking back on today, two things I am proud of are...

Waking up before 8 am this morning.

Got the job I applied for 3 weeks ago.

My favorite moment of today was...

Reading together with my 3-year old son before his bedtime.

(Now close your eyes and take 1 full minute to relive that moment in your mind)

Someone who showed me kindness today was...

The guy who gave me the dollar I was short on at the checkout.

How will I make tomorrow better?

Leave a thank you note on my coworker's desk.

DATE _____ / _____ / 20 _____

The smallest act of kindness is worth more than the grandest intention.
- OSCAR WILDE

I am...

1. _____
2. _____
3. _____

Looking back on today, 2 amazing things I am proud of are...

1. _____
2. _____

My favorite moment of today was...

_____

(Now close your eyes and take 1 full minute to relive that moment in your mind)

Someone who showed me kindness today was...

_____

_____

How will I make tomorrow better?

_____

_____

DATE _____ / _____ / 20 _____

Forgiveness is a virtue of the brave.
- INDIRA GANDHI

I am...

1. _____
2. _____
3. _____

Looking back on today, 2 amazing things I am proud of are...

1. _____
2. _____

My favorite moment of today was...

_____

(Now close your eyes and take 1 full minute to relive that moment in your mind)

Someone who showed me kindness today was...

_____

_____

How will I make tomorrow better?

_____

_____

DATE _____ / _____ / 20 _____

I was always looking outside myself for strength and confidence,
but it comes from within.
- ANNA FREUD

I am...

1. _____
2. _____
3. _____

Looking back on today, 2 amazing things I am proud of are...

1. _____
2. _____

My favorite moment of today was...

_____
(Now close your eyes and take 1 full minute to relive that moment in your mind)

Someone who showed me kindness today was...

_____
_____

How will I make tomorrow better?

_____
_____

DATE _____ / _____ / 20 _____

Your big opportunity may be right where you are now.
- NAPOLEON HILL

I am...

1. _____
2. _____
3. _____

Looking back on today, 2 amazing things I am proud of are...

1. _____
2. _____

My favorite moment of today was...

_____

(Now close your eyes and take 1 full minute to relive that moment in your mind)

Someone who showed me kindness today was...

_____

_____

How will I make tomorrow better?

_____

_____

DATE _____ / _____ / 20 _____

Friendship is born at that moment when one person says to another:
'What! You too? I thought I was the only one'.
- C.S. LEWIS

I am...

1. _____
2. _____
3. _____

Looking back on today, 2 amazing things I am proud of are...

1. _____
2. _____

My favorite moment of today was...

_____

(Now close your eyes and take 1 full minute to relive that moment in your mind)

Someone who showed me kindness today was...

_____

_____

How will I make tomorrow better?

_____

_____

44

DATE _____ / _____ / 20 _____

Forgiveness doesn't mean saying "yes" to what someone did.
It means saying "no" to the anger inside you over it.
- NATASHA SHARMA

I am...

1. _____
2. _____
3. _____

Looking back on today, 2 amazing things I am proud of are...

1. _____
2. _____

My favorite moment of today was...

_____

(Now close your eyes and take 1 full minute to relive that moment in your mind)

Someone who showed me kindness today was...

_____

_____

How will I make tomorrow better?

_____

_____

DATE _____ / _____ / 20 _____

WEEKLY DARE
Give a compliment to a stranger.

I am...

1. _____
2. _____
3. _____

Looking back on today, 2 amazing things I am proud of are...

1. _____
2. _____

My favorite moment of today was...

_____

(Now close your eyes and take 1 full minute to relive that moment in your mind)

Someone who showed me kindness today was...

_____

_____

How will I make tomorrow better?

_____

_____

DATE _____ / _____ / 20 _____

You must be the change you wish to see in the world.
- MAHATMA GHANDI

I am...

1. _____
2. _____
3. _____

Looking back on today, 2 amazing things I am proud of are...

1. _____
2. _____

My favorite moment of today was...

_____

(Now close your eyes and take 1 full minute to relive that moment in your mind)

Someone who showed me kindness today was...

_____

_____

How will I make tomorrow better?

_____

_____

DATE _____ / _____ / 20 _____

Not all those who wander are lost.
- J.R.R. TOLKIEN

I am...

1. _____
2. _____
3. _____

Looking back on today, 2 amazing things I am proud of are...

1. _____
2. _____

My favorite moment of today was...

_____
(Now close your eyes and take 1 full minute to relive that moment in your mind)

Someone who showed me kindness today was...

_____

_____

How will I make tomorrow better?

_____

_____

DATE _____ / _____ / 20 _____

You miss 100% of the shots you don't take.
- WAYNE GRETZKY

I am...

1. _____
2. _____
3. _____

Looking back on today, 2 amazing things I am proud of are...

1. _____
2. _____

My favorite moment of today was...

_____

(Now close your eyes and take 1 full minute to relive that moment in your mind)

Someone who showed me kindness today was...

_____

_____

How will I make tomorrow better?

_____

_____

DATE _____ / _____ / 20 _____

Your life does not get better by chance, it gets better by change.
- JIM ROHN

I am...

1. _____
2. _____
3. _____

Looking back on today, 2 amazing things I am proud of are...

1. _____
2. _____

My favorite moment of today was...

_____

(Now close your eyes and take 1 full minute to relive that moment in your mind)

Someone who showed me kindness today was...

_____

_____

How will I make tomorrow better?

_____

_____

DATE _____ / _____ / 20 _____

You cannot be lonely if you like the person you're alone with.
- DR. WAYNE DYER

I am...

1. _____
2. _____
3. _____

Looking back on today, 2 amazing things I am proud of are...

1. _____
2. _____

My favorite moment of today was...

_____

(Now close your eyes and take 1 full minute to relive that moment in your mind)

Someone who showed me kindness today was...

_____

_____

How will I make tomorrow better?

_____

_____

DATE _____ / _____ / 20 _____

Be silly sometimes. It makes life more fun.
- NATASHA SHARMA

I am...

1. _____
2. _____
3. _____

Looking back on today, 2 amazing things I am proud of are...

1. _____
2. _____

My favorite moment of today was...

_____

(Now close your eyes and take 1 full minute to relive that moment in your mind)

Someone who showed me kindness today was...

_____

_____

How will I make tomorrow better?

_____

_____

DATE _____ / _____ / 20 _____

WEEKLY DARE
Look at yourself in the mirror, keeping eye contact, for 30 seconds.

I am...

1. _____
2. _____
3. _____

Looking back on today, 2 amazing things I am proud of are...

1. _____
2. _____

My favorite moment of today was...

_____

(Now close your eyes and take 1 full minute to relive that moment in your mind)

Someone who showed me kindness today was...

_____

_____

How will I make tomorrow better?

_____

_____

DATE _____ / _____ / 20 _____

There is more to life than increasing its speed.
- MAHATMA GANDHI

I am...

1. _____
2. _____
3. _____

Looking back on today, 2 amazing things I am proud of are...

1. _____
2. _____

My favorite moment of today was...

_____

(Now close your eyes and take 1 full minute to relive that moment in your mind)

Someone who showed me kindness today was...

_____

_____

How will I make tomorrow better?

_____

_____

DATE _____ / _____ / 20 _____

You can always, always give something, even if it is only kindness.
- ANNE FRANK

I am...

1. _____
2. _____
3. _____

Looking back on today, 2 amazing things I am proud of are...

1. _____
2. _____

My favorite moment of today was...

_____

(Now close your eyes and take 1 full minute to relive that moment in your mind)

Someone who showed me kindness today was...

_____
_____

How will I make tomorrow better?

_____
_____

DATE _____ / _____ / 20 _____

To be happy, we must not be too concerned with others.
- ALBERT CAMUS

I am...

1. _____
2. _____
3. _____

Looking back on today, 2 amazing things I am proud of are...

1. _____
2. _____

My favorite moment of today was...

_____

(Now close your eyes and take 1 full minute to relive that moment in your mind)

Someone who showed me kindness today was...

_____

_____

How will I make tomorrow better?

_____

_____

DATE _____ / _____ / 20 _____

Wishing for the life you could have will rob you of the life you do have.
- NATASHA SHARMA

I am...

1. _____
2. _____
3. _____

Looking back on today, 2 amazing things I am proud of are...

1. _____
2. _____

My favorite moment of today was...

_____

(Now close your eyes and take 1 full minute to relive that moment in your mind)

Someone who showed me kindness today was...

_____

_____

How will I make tomorrow better?

_____

_____

DATE _____ / _____ / 20 _____

*"One who knows how to show and to accept kindness will be
a friend better than any possession."*
- SOPHOCLES

I am...

1. _____
2. _____
3. _____

Looking back on today, 2 amazing things I am proud of are...

1. _____
2. _____

My favorite moment of today was...

_____

(Now close your eyes and take 1 full minute to relive that moment in your mind)

Someone who showed me kindness today was...

_____

_____

How will I make tomorrow better?

_____

_____

DATE _____ / _____ / 20 _____

Whoever is happy will make others happy too.
- ANNE FRANK

I am...

1. _____
2. _____
3. _____

Looking back on today, 2 amazing things I am proud of are...

1. _____
2. _____

My favorite moment of today was...

_____

(Now close your eyes and take 1 full minute to relive that moment in your mind)

Someone who showed me kindness today was...

_____

_____

How will I make tomorrow better?

_____

_____

DATE _____ / _____ / 20 _____

WEEKLY DARE
Start a conversation with someone you don't know.

I am...

1. _____
2. _____
3. _____

Looking back on today, 2 amazing things I am proud of are...

1. _____
2. _____

My favorite moment of today was...

_____

(Now close your eyes and take 1 full minute to relive that moment in your mind)

Someone who showed me kindness today was...

_____

_____

How will I make tomorrow better?

_____

_____

DATE _____ / _____ / 20 _____

When being together is more important than what you do,
you are with a friend.
- CONNIE McMARTIN

I am...

1. _____
2. _____
3. _____

Looking back on today, 2 amazing things I am proud of are...

1. _____
2. _____

My favorite moment of today was...

_____

(Now close your eyes and take 1 full minute to relive that moment in your mind)

Someone who showed me kindness today was...

_____

_____

How will I make tomorrow better?

_____

_____

DATE _____ / _____ / 20 _____

The best preparation for tomorrow is doing your best today.
- H. JACKSON BROWN JR.

I am...

1. _____
2. _____
3. _____

Looking back on today, 2 amazing things I am proud of are...

1. _____
2. _____

My favorite moment of today was...

_____

(Now close your eyes and take 1 full minute to relive that moment in your mind)

Someone who showed me kindness today was...

_____

_____

How will I make tomorrow better?

_____

_____

DATE _____ / _____ / 20 _____

When you say 'yes' to others, make sure you aren't saying 'no' to yourself.
- PAULO COELHO

I am...

1. _____
2. _____
3. _____

Looking back on today, 2 amazing things I am proud of are...

1. _____
2. _____

My favorite moment of today was...

_____

(Now close your eyes and take 1 full minute to relive that moment in your mind)

Someone who showed me kindness today was...

_____
_____

How will I make tomorrow better?

_____
_____

DATE _____ / _____ / 20 _____

The happiness of your life depends upon the quality of your thoughts;
therefore guard accordingly.
- MARCUS AURELIUS

I am...

1. _____
2. _____
3. _____

Looking back on today, 2 amazing things I am proud of are...

1. _____
2. _____

My favorite moment of today was...

_____

(Now close your eyes and take 1 full minute to relive that moment in your mind)

Someone who showed me kindness today was...

_____

_____

How will I make tomorrow better?

_____

_____

DATE _____ / _____ / 20 _____

We are the stories we tell.
- SUSAN GREGORY THOMAS

I am...

1. _____
2. _____
3. _____

Looking back on today, 2 amazing things I am proud of are...

1. _____
2. _____

My favorite moment of today was...

_____

(Now close your eyes and take 1 full minute to relive that moment in your mind)

Someone who showed me kindness today was...

_____

_____

How will I make tomorrow better?

_____

_____

DATE _____ / _____ / 20 _____

You can't lead a cavalry charge if you think you look funny on a horse.
- JOHN PEERS

I am...

1. _____
2. _____
3. _____

Looking back on today, 2 amazing things I am proud of are...

1. _____
2. _____

My favorite moment of today was...

_____

(Now close your eyes and take 1 full minute to relive that moment in your mind)

Someone who showed me kindness today was...

_____

_____

How will I make tomorrow better?

_____

_____

DATE _____ / _____ / 20 _____

WEEKLY DARE
Write a letter to yourself aged one year ago from today.
What advice would you give?

I am...

1. _____
2. _____
3. _____

Looking back on today, 2 amazing things I am proud of are...

1. _____
2. _____

My favorite moment of today was...

_____

(Now close your eyes and take 1 full minute to relive that moment in your mind)

Someone who showed me kindness today was...

_____
_____

How will I make tomorrow better?

_____
_____

DATE _____ / _____ / 20 _____

Don't call it a dream. Call it a plan.
- UNKNOWN

I am...

1. _____
2. _____
3. _____

Looking back on today, 2 amazing things I am proud of are...

1. _____
2. _____

My favorite moment of today was...

_____

(Now close your eyes and take 1 full minute to relive that moment in your mind)

Someone who showed me kindness today was...

_____

_____

How will I make tomorrow better?

_____

_____

DATE _____ / _____ / 20 _____

We make a living by what we get. We make a life by what we give.
- SIR WINSTON CHURCHILL

I am...

1. _____
2. _____
3. _____

Looking back on today, 2 amazing things I am proud of are...

1. _____
2. _____

My favorite moment of today was...

_____

(Now close your eyes and take 1 full minute to relive that moment in your mind)

Someone who showed me kindness today was...

_____

_____

How will I make tomorrow better?

_____

_____

DATE _____ / _____ / 20 _____

Giving connects two people, the giver and the receiver.
- DEEPAK CHOPRA

I am...

1. _____
2. _____
3. _____

Looking back on today, 2 amazing things I am proud of are...

1. _____
2. _____

My favorite moment of today was...

_____

(Now close your eyes and take 1 full minute to relive that moment in your mind)

Someone who showed me kindness today was...

_____

_____

How will I make tomorrow better?

_____

_____

DATE _____ / _____ / 20 _____

We can choose to be affected by the world or
we can choose to affect the world.
- HEIDI WILLS

I am...

1. _____
2. _____
3. _____

Looking back on today, 2 amazing things I am proud of are...

1. _____
2. _____

My favorite moment of today was...

_____
(Now close your eyes and take 1 full minute to relive that moment in your mind)

Someone who showed me kindness today was...

_____
_____

How will I make tomorrow better?

_____
_____

DATE _____ / _____ / 20 _____

Have fun, be crazy, be weird.
- ANTHONY ROBBINS

I am...

1. _____
2. _____
3. _____

Looking back on today, 2 amazing things I am proud of are...

1. _____
2. _____

My favorite moment of today was...

_____

(Now close your eyes and take 1 full minute to relive that moment in your mind)

Someone who showed me kindness today was...

_____

_____

How will I make tomorrow better?

_____

_____

DATE _____ / _____ / 20 _____

Hope to leave the world a bit better than when you got here.
- JIM HENSON

I am...

1. _____
2. _____
3. _____

Looking back on today, 2 amazing things I am proud of are...

1. _____
2. _____

My favorite moment of today was...

_____

(Now close your eyes and take 1 full minute to relive that moment in your mind)

Someone who showed me kindness today was...

_____

_____

How will I make tomorrow better?

_____

_____

DATE _____ / _____ / 20 _____

WEEKLY DARE
Do not use technology (cellphones, computers, etc.) for one day.

I am...

1. _____
2. _____
3. _____

Looking back on today, 2 amazing things I am proud of are...

1. _____
2. _____

My favorite moment of today was...

_____

(Now close your eyes and take 1 full minute to relive that moment in your mind)

Someone who showed me kindness today was...

_____

_____

How will I make tomorrow better?

_____

_____

DATE _____ / _____ / 20 _____

We are what we repeatedly do. Excellence, therefore,
is not an act but a habit.
- ARISTOTLE

I am...

1. _____
2. _____
3. _____

Looking back on today, 2 amazing things I am proud of are...

1. _____
2. _____

My favorite moment of today was...

_____

(Now close your eyes and take 1 full minute to relive that moment in your mind)

Someone who showed me kindness today was...

_____

_____

How will I make tomorrow better?

_____

_____

DATE _____ / _____ / 20 _____

How beautiful a day can be when kindness touches it!
- GEORGE ELLISTON

I am...

1. _____
2. _____
3. _____

Looking back on today, 2 amazing things I am proud of are...

1. _____
2. _____

My favorite moment of today was...

_____

(Now close your eyes and take 1 full minute to relive that moment in your mind)

Someone who showed me kindness today was...

_____

_____

How will I make tomorrow better?

_____

_____

DATE _____ / _____ / 20 _____

Kindness is the language which the deaf can hear and the blind can see.
- MARK TWAIN

I am...

1. _____
2. _____
3. _____

Looking back on today, 2 amazing things I am proud of are...

1. _____
2. _____

My favorite moment of today was...

_____

(Now close your eyes and take 1 full minute to relive that moment in your mind)

Someone who showed me kindness today was...

_____

_____

How will I make tomorrow better?

_____

_____

DATE _____ / _____ / 20 _____

Three things in life are important. The first is to be kind.
The second is to be kind. And the third is to be kind.
- HENRY JAMES

I am...

1. _____
2. _____
3. _____

Looking back on today, 2 amazing things I am proud of are...

1. _____
2. _____

My favorite moment of today was...

_____

(Now close your eyes and take 1 full minute to relive that moment in your mind)

Someone who showed me kindness today was...

_____

_____

How will I make tomorrow better?

_____

_____

DATE _____ / _____ / 20 _____

Wherever there is a human being, there is an opportunity for kindness.
- LUCIUS ANNAEUS SENECA

I am...

1. _____
2. _____
3. _____

Looking back on today, 2 amazing things I am proud of are...

1. _____
2. _____

My favorite moment of today was...

_____

(Now close your eyes and take 1 full minute to relive that moment in your mind)

Someone who showed me kindness today was...

_____
_____

How will I make tomorrow better?

_____
_____

DATE _____ / _____ / 20 _____

The best way to predict the future is to create it.
- PETER DRUCKER

I am...

1. _____
2. _____
3. _____

Looking back on today, 2 amazing things I am proud of are...

1. _____
2. _____

My favorite moment of today was...

_____

(Now close your eyes and take 1 full minute to relive that moment in your mind)

Someone who showed me kindness today was...

_____

_____

How will I make tomorrow better?

_____

_____

DATE _____ / _____ / 20 _____

WEEKLY DARE
Eat one fuit or one vegetable with every meal for a day.

I am...

1. _____
2. _____
3. _____

Looking back on today, 2 amazing things I am proud of are...

1. _____
2. _____

My favorite moment of today was...

_____

(Now close your eyes and take 1 full minute to relive that moment in your mind)

Someone who showed me kindness today was...

_____

_____

How will I make tomorrow better?

_____

_____

DATE _____ / _____ / 20 _____

Always go with your passions. Never ask yourself if it's realistic or not.
- DEEPAK CHOPRA

I am...

1. _____
2. _____
3. _____

Looking back on today, 2 amazing things I am proud of are...

1. _____
2. _____

My favorite moment of today was...

_____

(Now close your eyes and take 1 full minute to relive that moment in your mind)

Someone who showed me kindness today was...

_____

_____

How will I make tomorrow better?

_____

_____

DATE _____ / _____ / 20 _____

Ambition is the path to success. Persistence is the vehicle you arrive in.
- BILL BRADLEY

I am...

1. _____
2. _____
3. _____

Looking back on today, 2 amazing things I am proud of are...

1. _____
2. _____

My favorite moment of today was...

_____

(Now close your eyes and take 1 full minute to relive that moment in your mind)

Someone who showed me kindness today was...

_____
_____

How will I make tomorrow better?

_____
_____

DATE _____ / _____ / 20 _____

Boredom is a space for conscious creativity. Don't fear it.
- NATASHA SHARMA

I am...

1. _____
2. _____
3. _____

Looking back on today, 2 amazing things I am proud of are...

1. _____
2. _____

My favorite moment of today was...

_____

(Now close your eyes and take 1 full minute to relive that moment in your mind)

Someone who showed me kindness today was...

_____

_____

How will I make tomorrow better?

_____

_____

DATE _____ / _____ / 20 _____

Comparison is the thief of joy.
- THEODORE ROOSEVELT

I am...

1. _____
2. _____
3. _____

Looking back on today, 2 amazing things I am proud of are...

1. _____
2. _____

My favorite moment of today was...

_____

(Now close your eyes and take 1 full minute to relive that moment in your mind)

Someone who showed me kindness today was...

_____

_____

How will I make tomorrow better?

_____

_____

DATE _____ / _____ / 20 _____

Do not wait; the time will never be "just right." Start where you stand.
- NAPOLEON HILL

I am...

1. _____
2. _____
3. _____

Looking back on today, 2 amazing things I am proud of are...

1. _____
2. _____

My favorite moment of today was...

_____

(Now close your eyes and take 1 full minute to relive that moment in your mind)

Someone who showed me kindness today was...

_____

_____

How will I make tomorrow better?

_____

_____

DATE _____ / _____ / 20 _____

Satisfaction is getting what you want. Happiness is wanting what you get.
- VARIOUS

I am...

1. _____
2. _____
3. _____

Looking back on today, 2 amazing things I am proud of are...

1. _____
2. _____

My favorite moment of today was...

_____

(Now close your eyes and take 1 full minute to relive that moment in your mind)

Someone who showed me kindness today was...

_____

_____

How will I make tomorrow better?

_____

_____

DATE _____ / _____ / 20 _____

WEEKLY DARE
Sing in the shower.

I am...

1. _____
2. _____
3. _____

Looking back on today, 2 amazing things I am proud of are...

1. _____
2. _____

My favorite moment of today was...

_____

(Now close your eyes and take 1 full minute to relive that moment in your mind)

Someone who showed me kindness today was...

_____

_____

How will I make tomorrow better?

_____

_____

DATE _____ / _____ / 20 _____

Dream big and dare to fail.
- NORMAN VAUGHAN

I am...

1. _____
2. _____
3. _____

Looking back on today, 2 amazing things I am proud of are...

1. _____
2. _____

My favorite moment of today was...

_____

(Now close your eyes and take 1 full minute to relive that moment in your mind)

Someone who showed me kindness today was...

_____

_____

How will I make tomorrow better?

_____

_____

DATE _____ / _____ / 20 _____

Enthusiasm moves the world.
- ARTHUR BALFOUR

I am...

1. _____
2. _____
3. _____

Looking back on today, 2 amazing things I am proud of are...

1. _____
2. _____

My favorite moment of today was...

_____

(Now close your eyes and take 1 full minute to relive that moment in your mind)

Someone who showed me kindness today was...

_____
_____

How will I make tomorrow better?

_____
_____

DATE _____ / _____ / 20 _____

Everybody laughs the same in every language
because laughter is a universal connection.
- YAKOV SMIRNOFF

I am...

1. _____
2. _____
3. _____

Looking back on today, 2 amazing things I am proud of are...

1. _____
2. _____

My favorite moment of today was...

_____

(Now close your eyes and take 1 full minute to relive that moment in your mind)

Someone who showed me kindness today was...

_____

_____

How will I make tomorrow better?

_____

_____

DATE _____ / _____ / 20 _____

Excellence is to do a common thing in an uncommon way.
- BOOKER T. WASHINGTON

I am...

1. _____
2. _____
3. _____

Looking back on today, 2 amazing things I am proud of are...

1. _____
2. _____

My favorite moment of today was...

_____

(Now close your eyes and take 1 full minute to relive that moment in your mind)

Someone who showed me kindness today was...

_____

_____

How will I make tomorrow better?

_____

_____

DATE _____ / _____ / 20 _____

Problems are not stop signs; they are guidelines.
- ROBER H. SCHULLER

I am...

1. _____
2. _____
3. _____

Looking back on today, 2 amazing things I am proud of are...

1. _____
2. _____

My favorite moment of today was...

_____

(Now close your eyes and take 1 full minute to relive that moment in your mind)

Someone who showed me kindness today was...

_____

_____

How will I make tomorrow better?

_____

_____

DATE _____ / _____ / 20 _____

Go ahead, reinvent the wheel. You may just discover how to fly.
- NATASHA SHARMA

I am...

1. _____
2. _____
3. _____

Looking back on today, 2 amazing things I am proud of are...

1. _____
2. _____

My favorite moment of today was...

_____

(Now close your eyes and take 1 full minute to relive that moment in your mind)

Someone who showed me kindness today was...

_____

_____

How will I make tomorrow better?

_____

_____

DATE _____ / _____ / 20 _____

WEEKLY DARE
Take a long walk with just yourself.

I am...

1. _____
2. _____
3. _____

Looking back on today, 2 amazing things I am proud of are...

1. _____
2. _____

My favorite moment of today was...

_____
(Now close your eyes and take 1 full minute to relive that moment in your mind)

Someone who showed me kindness today was...

_____
_____

How will I make tomorrow better?

_____
_____

DATE _____ / _____ / 20 _____

Great opportunities to help others seldom come, but small ones come daily.
- IVY BAKER PRIEST

I am...

1. _____
2. _____
3. _____

Looking back on today, 2 amazing things I am proud of are...

1. _____
2. _____

My favorite moment of today was...

_____
(Now close your eyes and take 1 full minute to relive that moment in your mind)

Someone who showed me kindness today was...

_____
_____

How will I make tomorrow better?

_____
_____

DATE _____ / _____ / 20 _____

Happiness comes of the capacity to feel deeply, to enjoy simply,
to think freely, to be needed.
- STORM JAMESON

I am...

1. _____
2. _____
3. _____

Looking back on today, 2 amazing things I am proud of are...

1. _____
2. _____

My favorite moment of today was...

_____

(Now close your eyes and take 1 full minute to relive that moment in your mind)

Someone who showed me kindness today was...

_____

_____

How will I make tomorrow better?

_____

_____

DATE _____ / _____ / 20 _____

Happiness depends upon ourselves.
- ARISTOTLE

I am...

1. _____
2. _____
3. _____

Looking back on today, 2 amazing things I am proud of are...

1. _____
2. _____

My favorite moment of today was...

_____

(Now close your eyes and take 1 full minute to relive that moment in your mind)

Someone who showed me kindness today was...

_____
_____

How will I make tomorrow better?

_____
_____

DATE _____ / _____ / 20 _____

Happiness is not a goal, but a by-product.
- ELEANOR ROOSEVELT

I am...

1. _____
2. _____
3. _____

Looking back on today, 2 amazing things I am proud of are...

1. _____
2. _____

My favorite moment of today was...

_____

(Now close your eyes and take 1 full minute to relive that moment in your mind)

Someone who showed me kindness today was...

_____

_____

How will I make tomorrow better?

_____

_____

DATE _____ / _____ / 20 _____

How wonderful it is that nobody need wait a single moment
before starting to improve the world.
- ANNE FRANK

I am...

1. _____
2. _____
3. _____

Looking back on today, 2 amazing things I am proud of are...

1. _____
2. _____

My favorite moment of today was...

_____

(Now close your eyes and take 1 full minute to relive that moment in your mind)

Someone who showed me kindness today was...

_____

_____

How will I make tomorrow better?

_____

_____

DATE _____ / _____ / 20 _____

I am a part of all that I have met.
- ALFRED LORD TENNYSON

I am...

1. _____
2. _____
3. _____

Looking back on today, 2 amazing things I am proud of are...

1. _____
2. _____

My favorite moment of today was...

_____

(Now close your eyes and take 1 full minute to relive that moment in your mind)

Someone who showed me kindness today was...

_____

_____

How will I make tomorrow better?

_____

_____

DATE _____ / _____ / 20 _____

WEEKLY DARE
Avoid using the word "should" for one day.

I am...

1. _____
2. _____
3. _____

Looking back on today, 2 amazing things I am proud of are...

1. _____
2. _____

My favorite moment of today was...

_____

(Now close your eyes and take 1 full minute to relive that moment in your mind)

Someone who showed me kindness today was...

_____
_____

How will I make tomorrow better?

_____
_____

DATE _____ / _____ / 20 _____

A simple Hello could lead to a million things.
- UNKNOWN

I am...

1. _____
2. _____
3. _____

Looking back on today, 2 amazing things I am proud of are...

1. _____
2. _____

My favorite moment of today was...

_____
(Now close your eyes and take 1 full minute to relive that moment in your mind)

Someone who showed me kindness today was...

_____
_____

How will I make tomorrow better?

_____
_____

DATE _____ / _____ / 20 _____

If opportunity doesn't knock, build a door.
- MILTON BERLE

I am...

1. _____
2. _____
3. _____

Looking back on today, 2 amazing things I am proud of are...

1. _____
2. _____

My favorite moment of today was...

_____

(Now close your eyes and take 1 full minute to relive that moment in your mind)

Someone who showed me kindness today was...

_____

_____

How will I make tomorrow better?

_____

_____

DATE _____ / _____ / 20 _____

If we did all the things we are capable of,
we would literally astound ourselves.
- THOMAS A. EDISON

I am...

1. _____
2. _____
3. _____

Looking back on today, 2 amazing things I am proud of are...

1. _____
2. _____

My favorite moment of today was...

_____

(Now close your eyes and take 1 full minute to relive that moment in your mind)

Someone who showed me kindness today was...

_____

_____

How will I make tomorrow better?

_____

_____

DATE _____ / _____ / 20 _____

If you can't do great things, do small things in a great way.
- NAPOLEON HILL

I am...

1. _____
2. _____
3. _____

Looking back on today, 2 amazing things I am proud of are...

1. _____
2. _____

My favorite moment of today was...

_____

(Now close your eyes and take 1 full minute to relive that moment in your mind)

Someone who showed me kindness today was...

_____
_____

How will I make tomorrow better?

_____
_____

DATE _____ / _____ / 20 _____

If you really want to do something, you'll find a way.
If you don't, you'll find an excuse.
- JIM ROHN

I am...

1. _____
2. _____
3. _____

Looking back on today, 2 amazing things I am proud of are...

1. _____
2. _____

My favorite moment of today was...

_____

(Now close your eyes and take 1 full minute to relive that moment in your mind)

Someone who showed me kindness today was...

_____

_____

How will I make tomorrow better?

_____

_____

DATE _____ / _____ / 20 _____

If your compassion does not include yourself, it is incomplete.
- BUDDHA

I am...

1. _____
2. _____
3. _____

Looking back on today, 2 amazing things I am proud of are...

1. _____
2. _____

My favorite moment of today was...

_____

(Now close your eyes and take 1 full minute to relive that moment in your mind)

Someone who showed me kindness today was...

_____

_____

How will I make tomorrow better?

_____

_____

DATE _____ / _____ / 20 _____

WEEKLY DARE
Call up a friend who you haven't spoken to in ages.

I am...

1. _____
2. _____
3. _____

Looking back on today, 2 amazing things I am proud of are...

1. _____
2. _____

My favorite moment of today was...

_____

(Now close your eyes and take 1 full minute to relive that moment in your mind)

Someone who showed me kindness today was...

_____

_____

How will I make tomorrow better?

_____

_____

DATE _____ / _____ / 20 _____

If opportunity doesn't knock, build a door.
- MILTON BERLE

I am...

1. _____
2. _____
3. _____

Looking back on today, 2 amazing things I am proud of are...

1. _____
2. _____

My favorite moment of today was...

_____

(Now close your eyes and take 1 full minute to relive that moment in your mind)

Someone who showed me kindness today was...

_____

_____

How will I make tomorrow better?

_____

_____

DATE _____ / _____ / 20 _____

In order to know if you're getting somewhere,
you need to know where you're going.
- NATASHA SHARMA

I am...

1. _____
2. _____
3. _____

Looking back on today, 2 amazing things I am proud of are...

1. _____
2. _____

My favorite moment of today was...

_____

(Now close your eyes and take 1 full minute to relive that moment in your mind)

Someone who showed me kindness today was...

_____

_____

How will I make tomorrow better?

_____

_____

DATE _____ / _____ / 20 _____

It is precisely the possibility of realizing a dream that makes life interesting.
- PAULO COELHO

I am...

1. _____
2. _____
3. _____

Looking back on today, 2 amazing things I am proud of are...

1. _____
2. _____

My favorite moment of today was...

_____

(Now close your eyes and take 1 full minute to relive that moment in your mind)

Someone who showed me kindness today was...

_____
_____

How will I make tomorrow better?

_____
_____

DATE _____ / _____ / 20 _____

It may be those who do most, dream most.
- STEPHEN LEACOCK

I am...

1. _____
2. _____
3. _____

Looking back on today, 2 amazing things I am proud of are...

1. _____
2. _____

My favorite moment of today was...

_____

(Now close your eyes and take 1 full minute to relive that moment in your mind)

Someone who showed me kindness today was...

_____

_____

How will I make tomorrow better?

_____

_____

113

DATE _____ / _____ / 20 _____

It's easier to go down a hill than up it, but the view is much better at the top.
- HENRY WARD BEECHER

I am...

1. _____
2. _____
3. _____

Looking back on today, 2 amazing things I am proud of are...

1. _____
2. _____

My favorite moment of today was...

_____
(Now close your eyes and take 1 full minute to relive that moment in your mind)

Someone who showed me kindness today was...

_____
_____

How will I make tomorrow better?

_____
_____

DATE _____ / _____ / 20 _____

Failure is success if we learn from it.
- MALCOLM FORBES

I am...

1. _____
2. _____
3. _____

Looking back on today, 2 amazing things I am proud of are...

1. _____
2. _____

My favorite moment of today was...

_____

(Now close your eyes and take 1 full minute to relive that moment in your mind)

Someone who showed me kindness today was...

_____

_____

How will I make tomorrow better?

_____

_____

DATE _____ / _____ / 20 _____

WEEKLY DARE
Give someone you love a random hug.

I am...

1. _____
2. _____
3. _____

Looking back on today, 2 amazing things I am proud of are...

1. _____
2. _____

My favorite moment of today was...

_____

(Now close your eyes and take 1 full minute to relive that moment in your mind)

Someone who showed me kindness today was...

_____

_____

How will I make tomorrow better?

_____

_____

DATE _____ / _____ / 20 _____

Live each day as if your life had just begun.
- JOHANN WOLFGANG VON GOETHE

I am...

1. _____
2. _____
3. _____

Looking back on today, 2 amazing things I am proud of are...

1. _____
2. _____

My favorite moment of today was...

_____

(Now close your eyes and take 1 full minute to relive that moment in your mind)

Someone who showed me kindness today was...

_____

_____

How will I make tomorrow better?

_____

_____

DATE _____ / _____ / 20 _____

If plan A didn't work, the alphabet has 25 more letters.
- UNKNOWN

I am...

1. _____
2. _____
3. _____

Looking back on today, 2 amazing things I am proud of are...

1. _____
2. _____

My favorite moment of today was...

_____

(Now close your eyes and take 1 full minute to relive that moment in your mind)

Someone who showed me kindness today was...

_____

_____

How will I make tomorrow better?

_____

_____

DATE _____ / _____ / 20 _____

The highest appreciation is not to utter words, but to live by them.
- JOHN F. KENNEDY

I am...

1. _____
2. _____
3. _____

Looking back on today, 2 amazing things I am proud of are...

1. _____
2. _____

My favorite moment of today was...

_____

(Now close your eyes and take 1 full minute to relive that moment in your mind)

Someone who showed me kindness today was...

_____

_____

How will I make tomorrow better?

_____

_____

DATE _____ / _____ / 20 _____

Take care of your body. It's the only place you have to live.
- JIM ROHN

I am...

1. _____
2. _____
3. _____

Looking back on today, 2 amazing things I am proud of are...

1. _____
2. _____

My favorite moment of today was...

_____

(Now close your eyes and take 1 full minute to relive that moment in your mind)

Someone who showed me kindness today was...

_____

_____

How will I make tomorrow better?

_____

_____

DATE _____ / _____ / 20 _____

We rise by lifting others.
- ROBERT INGERSOLL

I am...

1. _____
2. _____
3. _____

Looking back on today, 2 amazing things I am proud of are...

1. _____
2. _____

My favorite moment of today was...

_____

(Now close your eyes and take 1 full minute to relive that moment in your mind)

Someone who showed me kindness today was...

_____

_____

How will I make tomorrow better?

_____

_____

DATE _____ / _____ / 20 _____

No act of kindness, no matter how small, is ever wasted.
- AESOP

I am...

1. _____
2. _____
3. _____

Looking back on today, 2 amazing things I am proud of are...

1. _____
2. _____

My favorite moment of today was...

_____

(Now close your eyes and take 1 full minute to relive that moment in your mind)

Someone who showed me kindness today was...

_____

_____

How will I make tomorrow better?

_____

_____

DATE _____ / _____ / 20 _____

WEEKLY DARE
Organize your most disorganized room or living space.

I am...

1. _____
2. _____
3. _____

Looking back on today, 2 amazing things I am proud of are...

1. _____
2. _____

My favorite moment of today was...

_____

(Now close your eyes and take 1 full minute to relive that moment in your mind)

Someone who showed me kindness today was...

_____

_____

How will I make tomorrow better?

_____

_____

DATE _____ / _____ / 20 _____

One must care about a world one will not see.
- BERTRAND RUSSELL

I am...

1. _____
2. _____
3. _____

Looking back on today, 2 amazing things I am proud of are...

1. _____
2. _____

My favorite moment of today was...

_____

(Now close your eyes and take 1 full minute to relive that moment in your mind)

Someone who showed me kindness today was...

_____

_____

How will I make tomorrow better?

_____

_____

DATE ____ / ____ / 20 ____

Overlearning leads to mastery.
- NATASHA SHARMA

I am...

1. _____
2. _____
3. _____

Looking back on today, 2 amazing things I am proud of are...

1. _____
2. _____

My favorite moment of today was...

_____

(Now close your eyes and take 1 full minute to relive that moment in your mind)

Someone who showed me kindness today was...

_____

_____

How will I make tomorrow better?

_____

_____

DATE _____ / _____ / 20 _____

Kindness is always fashionable.
- AMELIA E. BARR

I am...

1. _____
2. _____
3. _____

Looking back on today, 2 amazing things I am proud of are...

1. _____
2. _____

My favorite moment of today was...

_____
(Now close your eyes and take 1 full minute to relive that moment in your mind)

Someone who showed me kindness today was...

_____
_____

How will I make tomorrow better?

_____
_____

DATE _____ / _____ / 20 _____

Put your heart, mind, and soul into even your smallest acts.
This is the secret of success.
- SWAMI SIVANANDA

I am...

1. _____
2. _____
3. _____

Looking back on today, 2 amazing things I am proud of are...

1. _____
2. _____

My favorite moment of today was...

_____

(Now close your eyes and take 1 full minute to relive that moment in your mind)

Someone who showed me kindness today was...

_____

_____

How will I make tomorrow better?

_____

_____

DATE _____ / _____ / 20 _____

Respect is love in plain clothes.
- FRANK BYRNES

I am...

1. _____
2. _____
3. _____

Looking back on today, 2 amazing things I am proud of are...

1. _____
2. _____

My favorite moment of today was...

_____

(Now close your eyes and take 1 full minute to relive that moment in your mind)

Someone who showed me kindness today was...

_____

_____

How will I make tomorrow better?

_____

_____

DATE _____ / _____ / 20 _____

Seize common occasions and make them great.
- ORISON SWETT MARDEN

I am...

1. _____
2. _____
3. _____

Looking back on today, 2 amazing things I am proud of are...

1. _____
2. _____

My favorite moment of today was...

_____
(Now close your eyes and take 1 full minute to relive that moment in your mind)

Someone who showed me kindness today was...

_____
_____

How will I make tomorrow better?

_____
_____

DATE _____ / _____ / 20 _____

WEEKLY DARE
Sit in silence with your eyes closed for 10 minutes.

I am...

1. _____
2. _____
3. _____

Looking back on today, 2 amazing things I am proud of are...

1. _____
2. _____

My favorite moment of today was...

_____

(Now close your eyes and take 1 full minute to relive that moment in your mind)

Someone who showed me kindness today was...

_____
_____

How will I make tomorrow better?

_____
_____

DATE _____ / _____ / 20 _____

*Someone is enjoying shade today because someone
planted a tree a long time ago.*
- WARREN BUFFETT

I am...

1. _____
2. _____
3. _____

Looking back on today, 2 amazing things I am proud of are...

1. _____
2. _____

My favorite moment of today was...

_____

(Now close your eyes and take 1 full minute to relive that moment in your mind)

Someone who showed me kindness today was...

_____

_____

How will I make tomorrow better?

_____

_____

DATE _____ / _____ / 20 _____

Sometimes it's not the strength but gentleness that cracks the hardest shells.
- RICHARD PAUL EVANS

I am...

1. _____
2. _____
3. _____

Looking back on today, 2 amazing things I am proud of are...

1. _____
2. _____

My favorite moment of today was...

_____
(Now close your eyes and take 1 full minute to relive that moment in your mind)

Someone who showed me kindness today was...

_____
_____

How will I make tomorrow better?

_____
_____

DATE _____ / _____ / 20 _____

Somewhere beyond right and wrong, there is a garden. I will meet you there.
- RUMI

I am...

1. _____
2. _____
3. _____

Looking back on today, 2 amazing things I am proud of are...

1. _____
2. _____

My favorite moment of today was...

_____

(Now close your eyes and take 1 full minute to relive that moment in your mind)

Someone who showed me kindness today was...

_____

_____

How will I make tomorrow better?

_____

_____

DATE _____ / _____ / 20 _____

Strive to be happy instead of right.
- NATASHA SHARMA

I am...

1. _____
2. _____
3. _____

Looking back on today, 2 amazing things I am proud of are...

1. _____
2. _____

My favorite moment of today was...

_____

(Now close your eyes and take 1 full minute to relive that moment in your mind)

Someone who showed me kindness today was...

_____

_____

How will I make tomorrow better?

_____

_____

DATE _____ / _____ / 20 _____

The quieter you become, the more you can hear.
- RAM DASS

I am...

1. _____
2. _____
3. _____

Looking back on today, 2 amazing things I am proud of are...

1. _____
2. _____

My favorite moment of today was...

_____

(Now close your eyes and take 1 full minute to relive that moment in your mind)

Someone who showed me kindness today was...

_____

_____

How will I make tomorrow better?

_____

_____

DATE _____ / _____ / 20 _____

The doors we open and close each day decide the lives we live.
- FLORA WHITTEMORE

I am...

1. _____
2. _____
3. _____

Looking back on today, 2 amazing things I am proud of are...

1. _____
2. _____

My favorite moment of today was...

_____

(Now close your eyes and take 1 full minute to relive that moment in your mind)

Someone who showed me kindness today was...

_____

_____

How will I make tomorrow better?

_____

_____

DATE _____ / _____ / 20 _____

WEEKLY DARE
Skip your feet on a busy street for one minute.

I am...

1. _____
2. _____
3. _____

Looking back on today, 2 amazing things I am proud of are...

1. _____
2. _____

My favorite moment of today was...

_____

(Now close your eyes and take 1 full minute to relive that moment in your mind)

Someone who showed me kindness today was...

_____

_____

How will I make tomorrow better?

_____

_____

DATE _____ / _____ / 20 _____

The meaning of life is to find your gift. The purpose of life is to give it away.
- PABLO PICASSO

I am...

1. _____
2. _____
3. _____

Looking back on today, 2 amazing things I am proud of are...

1. _____
2. _____

My favorite moment of today was...

_____

(Now close your eyes and take 1 full minute to relive that moment in your mind)

Someone who showed me kindness today was...

_____

_____

How will I make tomorrow better?

_____

_____

DATE _____ / _____ / 20 _____

Always laugh when you can. It is cheap medicine.
- LORD BYRON

I am...

1. _____
2. _____
3. _____

Looking back on today, 2 amazing things I am proud of are...

1. _____
2. _____

My favorite moment of today was...

_____

(Now close your eyes and take 1 full minute to relive that moment in your mind)

Someone who showed me kindness today was...

_____

_____

How will I make tomorrow better?

_____

_____

DATE _____ / _____ / 20 _____

The power of imagination makes us infinite.
- JOHN MUIR

I am...

1. _____
2. _____
3. _____

Looking back on today, 2 amazing things I am proud of are...

1. _____
2. _____

My favorite moment of today was...

_____

(Now close your eyes and take 1 full minute to relive that moment in your mind)

Someone who showed me kindness today was...

_____

_____

How will I make tomorrow better?

_____

_____

DATE _____ / _____ / 20 _____

The privilege of a lifetime is being who you are.
- JOSEPH CAMPBELL

I am...

1. _____
2. _____
3. _____

Looking back on today, 2 amazing things I am proud of are...

1. _____
2. _____

My favorite moment of today was...

_____

(Now close your eyes and take 1 full minute to relive that moment in your mind)

Someone who showed me kindness today was...

_____

_____

How will I make tomorrow better?

_____

_____

DATE _____ / _____ / 20 _____

The secret of getting ahead is getting started.
- MARK TWAIN

I am...

1. _____
2. _____
3. _____

Looking back on today, 2 amazing things I am proud of are...

1. _____
2. _____

My favorite moment of today was...

_____

(Now close your eyes and take 1 full minute to relive that moment in your mind)

Someone who showed me kindness today was...

_____

_____

How will I make tomorrow better?

_____

_____

DATE _____ / _____ / 20 _____

The true essence of humankind is kindness.
- TENZIN GYATSO

I am...

1. _____
2. _____
3. _____

Looking back on today, 2 amazing things I am proud of are...

1. _____
2. _____

My favorite moment of today was...

_____

(Now close your eyes and take 1 full minute to relive that moment in your mind)

Someone who showed me kindness today was...

_____

_____

How will I make tomorrow better?

_____

_____

DATE _____ / _____ / 20 _____

WEEKLY DARE
Go to a movie or eat a meal by yourself (no phones, books, etc.)

I am...

1. _____
2. _____
3. _____

Looking back on today, 2 amazing things I am proud of are...

1. _____
2. _____

My favorite moment of today was...

_____

(Now close your eyes and take 1 full minute to relive that moment in your mind)

Someone who showed me kindness today was...

_____
_____

How will I make tomorrow better?

_____
_____

DATE _____ / _____ / 20 _____

Those who make compassion an essential part of
their lives find the joy of life.
- ROBERT J. FUREY

I am...

1. _____
2. _____
3. _____

Looking back on today, 2 amazing things I am proud of are...

1. _____
2. _____

My favorite moment of today was...

_____

(Now close your eyes and take 1 full minute to relive that moment in your mind)

Someone who showed me kindness today was...

_____

_____

How will I make tomorrow better?

_____

_____

DATE _____ / _____ / 20 _____

Time is the most valuable thing a man can spend.
- DIOGENES LAERTIUS

I am...

1. _____
2. _____
3. _____

Looking back on today, 2 amazing things I am proud of are...

1. _____
2. _____

My favorite moment of today was...

_____

(Now close your eyes and take 1 full minute to relive that moment in your mind)

Someone who showed me kindness today was...

_____

_____

How will I make tomorrow better?

_____

_____

DATE _____ / _____ / 20 _____

Today you are You, that is truer than true.
There is no one alive who is Youer than You.
- THEODOR SEUSS GEISEL

I am...

1. _____
2. _____
3. _____

Looking back on today, 2 amazing things I am proud of are...

1. _____
2. _____

My favorite moment of today was...

_____

(Now close your eyes and take 1 full minute to relive that moment in your mind)

Someone who showed me kindness today was...

_____

_____

How will I make tomorrow better?

_____

_____

DATE _____ / _____ / 20 _____

Try not to become a man of success but a man of value.
- ALBERT EINSTEIN

I am...

1. _____
2. _____
3. _____

Looking back on today, 2 amazing things I am proud of are...

1. _____
2. _____

My favorite moment of today was...

_____

(Now close your eyes and take 1 full minute to relive that moment in your mind)

Someone who showed me kindness today was...

_____

_____

How will I make tomorrow better?

_____

_____

DATE _____ / _____ / 20 _____

Dream big and dare to fail.
- NORMAN VAUGHAN

I am...

1. _____
2. _____
3. _____

Looking back on today, 2 amazing things I am proud of are...

1. _____
2. _____

My favorite moment of today was...

_____

(Now close your eyes and take 1 full minute to relive that moment in your mind)

Someone who showed me kindness today was...

_____

_____

How will I make tomorrow better?

_____

_____

DATE _____ / _____ / 20 _____

Try to be a rainbow in someone's cloud.
- MAYA ANGELOU

I am...

1. _____
2. _____
3. _____

Looking back on today, 2 amazing things I am proud of are...

1. _____
2. _____

My favorite moment of today was...

_____

(Now close your eyes and take 1 full minute to relive that moment in your mind)

Someone who showed me kindness today was...

_____
_____

How will I make tomorrow better?

_____
_____

DATE _____ / _____ / 20 _____

WEEKLY DARE
Tell someone close to you something nobody knows about you.

I am...

1. _____
2. _____
3. _____

Looking back on today, 2 amazing things I am proud of are...

1. _____
2. _____

My favorite moment of today was...

_____

(Now close your eyes and take 1 full minute to relive that moment in your mind)

Someone who showed me kindness today was...

_____

_____

How will I make tomorrow better?

_____

_____

DATE _____ / _____ / 20 _____

Motivation is what gets you started. Habit is what keeps you going.
- JIM ROHN

I am...

1. _____
2. _____
3. _____

Looking back on today, 2 amazing things I am proud of are...

1. _____
2. _____

My favorite moment of today was...

_____

(Now close your eyes and take 1 full minute to relive that moment in your mind)

Someone who showed me kindness today was...

_____

_____

How will I make tomorrow better?

_____

_____

DATE _____ / _____ / 20 _____

The future belongs to those who believe in the beauty of their dreams.
- ELEANOR ROOSEVELT

I am...

1. _____
2. _____
3. _____

Looking back on today, 2 amazing things I am proud of are...

1. _____
2. _____

My favorite moment of today was...

_____
(Now close your eyes and take 1 full minute to relive that moment in your mind)

Someone who showed me kindness today was...

_____
_____

How will I make tomorrow better?

_____
_____

DATE _____ / _____ / 20 _____

The hardest thing will be starting and finishing. In between is the easy part.
- NATASHA SHARMA

I am...

1. _____
2. _____
3. _____

Looking back on today, 2 amazing things I am proud of are...

1. _____
2. _____

My favorite moment of today was...

_____

(Now close your eyes and take 1 full minute to relive that moment in your mind)

Someone who showed me kindness today was...

_____

_____

How will I make tomorrow better?

_____

_____

DATE _____ / _____ / 20 _____

Nothing great was ever achieved without enthusiasm.
- RALPH WALDO EMERSON

I am...

1. _____
2. _____
3. _____

Looking back on today, 2 amazing things I am proud of are...

1. _____
2. _____

My favorite moment of today was...

_____

(Now close your eyes and take 1 full minute to relive that moment in your mind)

Someone who showed me kindness today was...

_____
_____

How will I make tomorrow better?

_____
_____

DATE _____ / _____ / 20 _____

Life isn't a matter of milestones, but of moments.
- ROSE KENNEDY

I am...

1. _____
2. _____
3. _____

Looking back on today, 2 amazing things I am proud of are...

1. _____
2. _____

My favorite moment of today was...

_____

(Now close your eyes and take 1 full minute to relive that moment in your mind)

Someone who showed me kindness today was...

_____

_____

How will I make tomorrow better?

_____

_____

DATE _____ / _____ / 20 _____

If you judge people, you have no time to love them.
- MOTHER THERESA

I am...

1. _____
2. _____
3. _____

Looking back on today, 2 amazing things I am proud of are...

1. _____
2. _____

My favorite moment of today was...

_____

(Now close your eyes and take 1 full minute to relive that moment in your mind)

Someone who showed me kindness today was...

_____

_____

How will I make tomorrow better?

_____

_____

DATE _____ / _____ / 20 _____

WEEKLY DARE
Wear something outrageous.

I am...

1. _____
2. _____
3. _____

Looking back on today, 2 amazing things I am proud of are...

1. _____
2. _____

My favorite moment of today was...

_____

(Now close your eyes and take 1 full minute to relive that moment in your mind)

Someone who showed me kindness today was...

_____
_____

How will I make tomorrow better?

_____
_____

DATE _____ / _____ / 20 _____

Gratitude is the best compliment, but action is the best messenger.
- NATASHA SHARMA

I am...

1. _____
2. _____
3. _____

Looking back on today, 2 amazing things I am proud of are...

1. _____
2. _____

My favorite moment of today was...

_____
(Now close your eyes and take 1 full minute to relive that moment in your mind)

Someone who showed me kindness today was...

_____
_____

How will I make tomorrow better?

_____
_____

DATE _____ / _____ / 20 _____

I didn't lose the gold. I won the silver.
- MICHELLE KWAN

I am...

1. _____
2. _____
3. _____

Looking back on today, 2 amazing things I am proud of are...

1. _____
2. _____

My favorite moment of today was...

_____

(Now close your eyes and take 1 full minute to relive that moment in your mind)

Someone who showed me kindness today was...

_____

_____

How will I make tomorrow better?

_____

_____

DATE _____ / _____ / 20 _____

Act like you expect to get into the end zone.
- CHRISTOPHER MORLEY

I am...

1. _____
2. _____
3. _____

Looking back on today, 2 amazing things I am proud of are...

1. _____
2. _____

My favorite moment of today was...

_____

(Now close your eyes and take 1 full minute to relive that moment in your mind)

Someone who showed me kindness today was...

_____

_____

How will I make tomorrow better?

_____

_____

DATE _____ / _____ / 20 _____

Every moment is a fresh beginning.
- T.S. ELIOT

I am...

1. _____
2. _____
3. _____

Looking back on today, 2 amazing things I am proud of are...

1. _____
2. _____

My favorite moment of today was...

_____

(Now close your eyes and take 1 full minute to relive that moment in your mind)

Someone who showed me kindness today was...

_____

_____

How will I make tomorrow better?

_____

_____

DATE _____ / _____ / 20 _____

Life begins at the end of your comfort zone.
- NEALE DONALD WALSCH

I am...

1. _____
2. _____
3. _____

Looking back on today, 2 amazing things I am proud of are...

1. _____
2. _____

My favorite moment of today was...

_____

(Now close your eyes and take 1 full minute to relive that moment in your mind)

Someone who showed me kindness today was...

_____

_____

How will I make tomorrow better?

_____

_____

DATE _____ / _____ / 20 _____

Starting strong is good. Finishing strong is epic.
- ROBIN SHARMA

I am...

1. _____
2. _____
3. _____

Looking back on today, 2 amazing things I am proud of are...

1. _____
2. _____

My favorite moment of today was...

_____
(Now close your eyes and take 1 full minute to relive that moment in your mind)

Someone who showed me kindness today was...

_____
_____

How will I make tomorrow better?

_____
_____

DATE _____ / _____ / 20 _____

WEEKLY DARE
Write a letter to yourself aged one year ahead from today.
What would you say?

I am...

1. _____
2. _____
3. _____

Looking back on today, 2 amazing things I am proud of are...

1. _____
2. _____

My favorite moment of today was...

_____

(Now close your eyes and take 1 full minute to relive that moment in your mind)

Someone who showed me kindness today was...

_____
_____

How will I make tomorrow better?

_____
_____

The Finish Line...
Just the Beginning

It's not the end of the book. It's the beginning of a new chapter. - **Unknown**

You've just completed a third of a year's worth of The Kindness Journal. Hats off to you! By now, writing in this journal should be firmly planted into your daily routine and you're likely reaping huge rewards in how you feel and view the world. I hope embarking on this journal has done for you what writing it - and writing in it - has done for me: To be and live well.

Take a moment to celebrate. You've earned it.

We hope you already have your next copy of the journal so that you can keep at it tomorrow and beyond.

If you'd like to share your experience with the journal, we'd love to hear from you! Please drop us a line at hi@thekindnessjournal.com or visit us at www.facebook.com/thekindnessjournal.

And remember: Don't stop here. This is just the beginning of what we hope will be a continuous journey toward your own personal growth and wellness.

References

1. Lyubomirsky, S., Sheldon, K.M., & Schkade, D. (2005).
   Pursuing Happiness: The architecture of sustainable
   change. *Review of General Psychology, Educational
   Publishing Foundation, Vol. 9, No. 2, 111-131*

2. Lyubomirsky, S., Sheldon, K.M., & Schkade, D. (2005).
   Pursuing Happiness: The architecture of sustainable
   change. *Review of General Psychology, Educational
   Publishing Foundation, Vol. 9, No. 2, 111-131*

3. Boehm, J.K., & Lyubomirsky, S. (2009). *The promise of
   sustainable happiness.* Oxford Handbook of Positive
   Psychology (2nd ed). New York, NY,
   Oxford University Press

4. Carney, D.R., Cuddy, A.J.C., & Yap, A.J. (2010).
   Power posing: Brief nonverbal displays affect
   neuroendocrine levels and risk tolerance.
   *Association for Psychological Science, 21 (10),
   1363-1368*

Acknowledgements

Thank you to my husband, best friend, and partner in crime Ladislav Beganyi, who has always encouraged and supported me to run with my ideas - even the crazy ones.

I'd also like to thank my sweet little boy Jay and Dane May you live and grow to be kind and compassionate people, to yourselves and to others.

Thank you as well to my amazing network of colleagues, writers, editors, and friends who read my notes, my manuscript drafts, and my relentless text messages late into the nights. You know who you are.

I would also like to thank some of the people who have taught and inspired me the most over my career: Vickie Beck (who wished for "More Kindness" in the world), Dr. Gloria Reeves and Dr. Daniel Rutley. Each of you has made a mark on my life.

Finally, thank you to all the people who I have worked with over the years as a therapist. Your resilience and tireless efforts toward self-improvement continue to inspire me long after our time is up.

About The Author

Natasha Sharma is a therapist, speaker, and TV/media personality. She received her Masters degree in Clinical Counseling from The Johns Hopkins University, and is about half way through her Doctorate degree in psychology at the time of publication. She's a regular columnist for a number of publications including YummyMummyClub.ca, InsideToronto.com, and TheBabySpot.ca. She also regularly appears on some of Canada's most popular TV shows including Global News Toronto, Breakfast Television, Entertainment Tonight, Etalk, and Rogers TV. Her tips and advice on personal wellness have been featured in The Globe and Mail and Huffington Post. She is devoted to helping others be their best and live their best by elevating themselves and transitioning to happier and more enjoyable lives.

www.natashasharma.com

Made in the USA
Middletown, DE
14 November 2020